What Brutes Men Are

A Comedy

Constance Cox

Samuel French — London
New York – Sydney – Toronto – Hollywood

CHARACTERS

Janet

Mildred
Carol
Linda

The action takes place in the lounge of a small, rather dingy country hotel

Time—the present

WHAT BRUTES MEN ARE

The lounge of a small country hotel. Mid-morning

At either side of the stage, there is a small drinks table with two chairs at each. Against the back wall is a larger table, on which dog-eared magazines are arranged, with a vase of wilted flowers between them. One or two easy chairs are against the walls, and the odd plant stand. There is a door which leads to the rest of the hotel

At one of the tables sits Janet. She is middle-aged, a little dowdy, but with a charming face and smile. The principal feature of her clothes is a rather flowery hat. There are coffee things on the table before her, and her coffee cup is half–full. She is glancing through a magazine. Mildred, the waitress, enters with a tray. She is about sixty, evidently an old retainer, and as such can be bossy and disapproving. She comes up to Janet

Mildred Will you be requiring anything more, madam?

Janet (*startled*) What? Oh, no, thank you.

Mildred Then I'll take your coffee things.

Janet No, leave them, please. I want another cup.

Mildred (*sternly*) We like to be finished with coffee by eleven-thirty, Mrs Talbot. You should know that.

Janet (*resigned*) Oh, all right. But let me pour out my last cup. Then you can take the other things away.

Mildred (*sighing heavily*) Very well, madam.

Janet, under her disapproving eye, hastily swallows the remains in her cup and pours out another. She is slightly clumsy in doing this because Mildred has made her nervous. As soon as she puts down the coffee-pot it is snatched away and put on the tray; likewise the milk jug and sugar-bowl. Mildred turns to depart

Janet You've taken the sugar . . .

Mildred goes to the door and exits, giving no sign of having heard Janet sighs, sips her coffee and makes a face. Then, resignedly, she puts down her cup and rises. She goes to the back table, replaces her magazine and sorts through the others. Finding one she has not read recently, she takes it and goes back to her seat, and leafs through the magazine

> *As soon as Janet is seated, Carol enters. She is about twenty-eight, pretty, and extremely smartly dressed. She carries a suitcase. She puts the suitcase down near the door, glances round as if looking for someone, then moves to sit at the vacant table. After a moment, she scrutinizes her watch, shakes it and puts it to her ear. She looks at it again, then looks across at Janet*

Carol Excuse me, what do you make the time?

Janet (*startled at being suddenly addressed*) The time? (*Looking at her watch*) Oh, eleven-thirty—just on.

Carol That's what I make it. Damn and blast!

Janet I beg your pardon?

Carol I hoped it was later. It's too early for a drink.

Janet Is it? I'm afraid I wouldn't know. I don't drink very much.

Carol Perhaps you've never needed to. Lucky you.

Janet Oh, I wouldn't say that. But why is eleven-thirty too early for a drink?

Carol Oh, it's just convention. The best people don't drink before midday, and then again not until the sun's over the yard-arm.

Janet How extraordinary!—How would they know?

Carol (*taking out a cigarette*) Know what?

Janet When the sun's over the yard-arm. Ordinary people, I mean. Not sailors.

Carol (*laughing*) Oh, it's just a saying. It means six o'clock.

Janet I see.

Carol But I'm damned if I'm waiting until midday or six o'clock tonight. I'm going to start now.—Do they have a waiter service in this hotel, or do I have to go to the bar?

Janet There is a *waitress* on duty. I expect she'll be here in a minute. She's got her eye on my coffee cup.

Carol I'm not waiting for anyone's convenience. I want service now.

> *Carol goes out determinedly*

Janet smiles and returns to her magazine

Carol returns after a couple of seconds

Janet (*looking up*) Any luck?
Carol Well, she caught my eye, if that means anything.
Janet It may or it may not.
Carol Like that, is it?
Janet Well, Mildred is a bit of a law unto herself.
Carol Is she? Then she'd better not cross me, because I'm in a bit of a steam-roller mood today. (*She goes to her table, only to find there is no ashtray*) I say, may I bag your ashtray, or do you need it? There isn't one here.
Janet Take it by all means. I don't smoke.
Carol (*picking up the ashtray and crossing with it to her table*) Would you say this was a reasonable hotel, or just plain ghastly? I'm sorry. You want to read and I keep interrupting you.
Janet It's all right. I was only passing the time. Anyway, I've seen all these magazines before.
Carol Like the ones . . . in dentists' waiting rooms, are they? Never changed.
Janet (*smiling*) Rather like that. What was it you asked? Oh, yes, about this hotel.
Carol It's pretty grisly by the look of it.
Janet I wouldn't say that. It's passable. It's come down over the years, of course. Are you thinking of staying here?
Carol I may have to. Just overnight. It depends. (*She wanders to the back table and touches the wilted flowers*)
Janet I think you'll be able to stand it for one night. The food's not bad. The Women's Luncheon Club comes here once a month.
Carol Is that a recommendation?
Janet Well, it's their day today, so the chef usually makes a special effort. As Secretary I try to make a point of it.
Carol (*amused*) So if I have lunch here today, the food will be slightly less revolting?
Janet (*smiling*) That's right. (*She glances towards the door*) Here's Mildred now if you want her.

Mildred enters. She goes straight to Janet's table and snatches up the cup

Mildred You *have* finished *now*, madam?

Janet (*after making a futile movement towards the cup*) Er—yes, thank you.

Mildred turns towards the door. Carol moves downstage

Carol Wait a minute. Don't you want to take my order?
Mildred (*frostily*) I wasn't aware that madam wished to order.
Carol I came out just now and beckoned to you.
Mildred Did you, madam? I'm afraid I didn't notice.
Carol I'd like a large gin-and-tonic, please.
Mildred (*going*) Yes, madam.
Carol And you might hover around a bit, because I shall probably need another.
Mildred (*repressively*) I have other people to see to, madam. I'll come when I can. (*She moves to the door*)
Carol Hang on,

Mildred sighs heavily

(*To Janet*) I say, will you join me?
Janet In a drink, you mean? Oh, no, thank you. I've only just had coffee.
Carol Oh, come on. To keep me company. It doesn't have to be gin. You could have a sherry.
Janet No, really, thank you. I shall have a glass of wine at lunch today, and that's about all I ever have.
Carol Just as you like. (*To Mildred*) Just the gin-and-tonic, then.
Mildred Yes, madam.

Mildred exits disapprovingly

Carol She's a real old sourpuss, isn't she? No wonder this place is going down if they're all like her. Why did you let her whisk your coffee away like that? I'd have snatched it back.
Janet I'm afraid Mildred takes advantage of the fact that she's known me for so many years. (*She looks around the room reminiscently*) My wedding reception was held here.
Carol What—in this dump?
Janet It was much nicer then.
Carol So I should hope.
Janet After all, it was over twenty years ago.
Carol Still, they might have put a coat of paint on it during all that time.

Janet smiles to herself

What's so funny?
Janet I was just remembering how Mildred managed to put me down even then.
Carol What, at your wedding reception?
Janet Yes—but you don't want to hear about it.
Carol (*sitting*) Yes, I do. Tell me.
Janet I was quite a young bride—only twenty-two and terribly nervous. At the end I had to stand up with my husband to cut the wedding cake. They gave me a big knife and I started to try and saw through the wretched thing. It was as hard as nails. I couldn't make any impression on it. Then Mildred hissed at me—she was standing just behind me—"You've only to make an incision, madam, then the waitresses take it away and cut it up." I blushed right down to my feet.
Carol The old devil! I bet she made sure everybody heard her.
Janet (*wryly*) I know they did.
Carol Well, she'd better not try any of her little tricks on me. I've just downed one tyrant, and I'm quite in the mood to take on another. Do I look peculiar?
Janet No. Just very nice.
Carol Isn't it odd when you think of it?
Janet Isn't what odd?
Carol How what we've done never *shows* on us. You'd think it would.
Janet What *have* you done?
Carol (*smiling*) Something terrific. Make a guess.
Janet Thrown up your job?
Carol You're not far off. I suppose you could call it a job in a sense.
Janet I'm quite sure you haven't robbed a bank.
Carol No. Try again.
Janet I can't . I give up.
Carol (*smiling*) I've walked out on my husband.
Janet (*appalled*) Oh, no! When?
Carol This very morning. At nine o'clock to be precise. I handed him his umbrella and his brief-case, saw him off to the station with a dutiful kiss, then skipped off.
Janet You mean—he doesn't know?
Carol Not yet. He will at six o'clock tonight. (*She walks about*

happily) I've left him a letter propped up on the drinks trolley.
It's the first place he'll go to when he gets home.
Janet You left him because he was a drunkard?
Carol Oh, no, he doesn't drink—well, only normally.
Janet Then why? It's such a serious step to take. Have you been
married very long?
Carol Eighteen months.
Janet That's a very short time, isn't it?
Carol I suppose it seems so to you. You've probably been married
for ages.
Janet I was. I'm not married any more.
Carol (*contritely*) Oh, I'm sorry. I shouldn't have—
Janet It's all right. I'm not a widow. I'm divorced.
Carol (*startled*) Divorced!
Janet (*smiling*) Why should it be so surprising?
Carol Well, you don't look like the divorcee type, somehow.
What happened? I bet you weren't the guilty party.
Janet Not in the legal sense.
Carol What other sense is there?
Janet I suppose you could say I let my husband down.
Carol (*standing by Janet's table*) I'm sure you didn't. Anyone
can see you must have been an ideal wife. Kind, thoughtful,
thoroughly domesticated—
Janet I tried to be. But none of those things count when one
isn't wanted any more.
Carol (*sitting at Janet's table*) What happened? You needn't
tell me if you don't want to.
Janet He said he'd fallen in love with someone else, and asked
me to release him. That's all.
Carol How dreadful for you! What brutes men are! Was it
long ago?
Janet It's a year and a half since the divorce became absolute.
He married her the next day.
Carol Isn't that typical? Just couldn't wait. How long were you
married?
Janet Over twenty years.
Carol Twenty years! That's nearly half a life-time.
Janet Yes.
Carol (*looking at her shrewdly*) I bet you're still in love with him.
Janet I don't know ... Yes, I think I am. (*Dreamily*) He was

so handsome, so go-ahead, so determined to make his way in the world . . . Is yours like that?

Carol Mine? Good lord, no! He's middle-aged, balding and he's got there. (*She looks round the dingy room*) And to think you still live in the town where you were married. You ought to have got away.

Janet I suppose I should have.

Carol Or do you still hope he may come back to you?

Janet I did at first. Now I shouldn't think there was the remotest chance.

Carol Well, thank goodness nothing like that can ever happen to me.

Mildred enters with the drink and a bottle of tonic water on a tray

Carol (*rising*) Ah, there you are. (*To Janet*) Are you sure you won't change your mind and have a drink?

Janet Well, perhaps I will. Talking about it has made me feel a bit melancholy.

Carol (*moving to her table*) What'll it be?

Janet Just a small sherry.

Carol (*to Mildred*) A small sherry. (*She opens her bag and puts a five-pound note on the tray*) And bring me another gin-and-tonic when you bring my change.

Mildred (*with an indescribable inflexion*) *Another*, madam? Very good, madam.

Mildred exits with a back like a ramrod

Carol (*chuckling*) She means very bad, madam. I don't think she approves of me at all. Do you think she'll have me chucked out?

Janet Not unless you create a disturbance, and I don't think you're likely to do that.

Carol (*pouring tonic into her glass*) You never know, the way I'm feeling.

Janet How are you feeling? A bit lost, perhaps?

Carol Good heavens, no! I'm feeling jubilant. I'm free! It feels marvellous. I want to paint the town red, set off fireworks— do something outrageous!

Janet You have already, I should say.

Carol What, leaving my husband? I ought to have my head
examined for not leaving him months ago. (*She picks up her
glass*) I say, may I bring this over to your table? It seems silly
to sit miles apart.

Janet Do.

Carol (*sitting at Janet's table*) There, that's more friendly.
(*Taking out her cigarettes*) Have one? Oh, you don't smoke,
you said.

Janet No, thank you.

Carol lights her cigarette

I suppose quite a number of things led up to your making this
decision.

Carol Oh, lots. But one puts up with the little things. I wasn't
fool enough to expect marriage to be a bed of roses.

Janet (*smiling*) It never is.

Carol No. It was living with his first wife all the time that finally
did it.

Janet His first wife?

Carol Didn't I tell you he'd been married before?

Janet No. You can't mean he actually made you share the same
house with her?

Carol No, of course not. (*She looks round for the ashtray, then
rises to collect it from her table, speaking as she goes*) In fact,
I don't think Godfrey had seen her since the day they were
divorced.

Janet Godfrey!

Carol (*returning with the ashtray*) Frightful name, isn't it? You
can't even abbreviate it. Soon after we were married, the
vicar came to see us. My husband was in the garden, and I
called out, "Oh, God, where are you?" The vicar thought I
was being blasphemous. (*She drinks*)

Janet Then—how did you mean that God . . . I mean—your
husband—made you share your home with his first wife?

Carol He simply recreated her. All the time. Believe me, that
woman shared our meals, sat on the sofa with us. I swear she's
even been in our bed.

Janet I can't help thinking you're exaggerating.

Carol Oh no, I'm not. You try having a model of perfection
held up to you all the time, and see if she doesn't pervade

the whole house. Well, now he can have his ruddy Janet back again, and good luck to him.

Janet (*faintly*) Janet—was that her name?

Carol Yes, and like Bloody Mary's Calais, it's graven on my heart.

Mildred enters with a small sherry on a tray, which she places by Janet

Ah, good, here's your drink. Where's my gin-and-tonic?

Mildred Madam only ordered sherry.

Carol Madam certainly did not. Madam ordered another gin-and-tonic and madam would like it pronto, if you please.

Mildred If you say so, madam.

Carol Madam does say so. You've got plenty of money there, haven't you?

Mildred Yes, madam, thank you. Enough, madam.

Sniffing, Mildred goes

Carol And three bags full, madam. Murder will be added to my other crimes before I leave here. (*She pours the remainder of the tonic into her glass*) Cheers.

Janet Cheers.

Carol No, I'd finally had enough. It's not as if I can't earn my own living again. I ran a boutique in Chelsea before I married, and I was jolly good at it.

Janet I'm sure you were.

Carol I simply had to go before I was thoroughly demoralized.

Janet Yes, I see . . . (*She sips her drink*) I'm awfully sorry if I seem rather dim, but did your Godfrey really hold up his first wife as a model of perfection all the time?

Carol Every day and twice on Sundays. Nothing but comparisons till they were practically coming out of my ears.

Janet Oh dear, oh dear, oh dear!

Carol You sound as if you know what I'm talking about.

Janet Only too well.

Carol According to Godfrey, she had all the virtues and then some. Never late, never ruffled, always the perfect hostess. Ran the house like clockwork, cooked like Escoffier, was beautiful as Helen of Troy, and dressed like a queen on tuppence ha'penny. After a time I began to wonder why he ever got rid of her.

Janet It does seem surprising. Did you ask him the reason?

Carol He said he fell in love with me. Simple as that.

Janet Probably because you were younger and prettier. After all, if they'd been married over twenty years.

Carol (*surprised*) I didn't say so, did I?

Janet (*unnerved*) Didn't you? I thought you did. (*To cover her confusion she looks at her watch*)

Carol Am I keeping you?

Janet Oh, no, no. The others won't be here for half an hour yet.

Carol Still, perhaps I'm boring you.

Janet On the contrary, I find all this fascinating. Rather horrific in a way. You see, all you've been describing is exactly what happened to me.

Carol You mean to say you married a horror like mine?

Janet Actually, I think I married the same horror. You're Carol Talbot, aren't you?

Carol Yes.

Janet Well, I'm Janet Talbot. Mrs Godfrey Talbot the First.

Carol But—you can't be!

Janet Why not?

Carol You aren't in the least like Godfrey said. I mean, you look awfully nice and kind and all that . . .

Janet But I'm not beautiful or smart or distinguished-looking. I quite agree. But I do assure you I'm Godfrey's first wife.

Carol Well, you could knock me down with a pole-axe.

Mildred enters with a gin-and-tonic

You've come just in time. I was going at the knees. Bring the same again.

Mildred (*appalled*) Again, madam!

Carol For both!

Mildred Both!

Janet Oh, not for me, please!

Carol Don't be silly. You need strong drink as much as I do.

Janet Then let me pay.

Carol Certainly not. You paid long enough. (*To Mildred*) Hang on to my change and tell me when you need some more.

Mildred (*breathing hard*) Very well, madam.

Mildred goes

Carol (*pouring the tonic into her gin*) You have a bash at that and you'll feel better. (*Passing the drink*) You know, I'm absolutely bewildered. No, I'm not. I'm ashamed.

Janet Ashamed? (*She starts on the gin-and-tonic*)

Carol To think that Godfrey and I between us should have done this to you.

Janet (*puzzled*) Done what to me?

Carol Well, I mean—to think that in eighteen months you should have changed so much. The divorce must have knocked you sideways.

Janet It did, of course, but . . .

Carol I can see you've *been* most awfully good-looking, but in your grief you've obviously let yourself go . . .

Janet I've done nothing of the kind. I'm exactly the same as I was when Godfrey left me. Eighteen months older, but that's all.

Carol You mean you were never—that is . . .

Janet I was never as beautiful as Helen of Troy, nor did I ever dress like a queen on tuppence ha'penny.

Carol Well, I'm jiggered!

Janet In fact, Godfrey frequently remarked that it was a waste of money buying clothes for me. He said anything I put on my back always looked as if it had been put through a mangle.

Carol looks puzzled

That's an old-fashioned thing they used to have before spin-dryers.

Carol But I swear to you he told me . . .

Janet Oh, I don't doubt you for a moment. I recognized the technique. (*She drinks*)

Carol Let me get this straight. What's your cooking like?

Janet Good and plain. Nothing fancy.

Carol Are you a perfect hostess?

Janet Not according to Godfrey. He always dined his clients out. The last thing he'd do was bring them home.

Carol In other words, he lied about you all along.

Janet I'm beginning to think he probably lied to us both. I see now it was his fiendish way of keeping us up to scratch.

Carol But he didn't compare you with anybody?

Janet Did he not! He never stopped. (*She drinks*)

Carol Wait a bit, you're going too fast for me.

Mildred enters with fresh drinks on her tray

And the service has speeded up as well. (*As Mildred puts the drinks down on the table*) The same again for you?

Janet Why not? (*She drains her glass*) No, this time I'd like a vodka. I've never had one.

Carol (*doubtfully*) I'm not sure how sherry, gin and vodka mix.

Janet (*cheerfully*) We'll find out then, won't we? Only let me pay for them.

Carol No fear. Not while it's still Godfrey's money. (*To Mildred*) Another gin, and a vodka-and-tonic. How's the cash situation?

Mildred (*frigidly*) I fancy there's just enough, madam.

Carol Good. Put it through the computer, will you?

Mildred casts her a viperish glance and goes

Janet (*giggling*) She'll get you before this is over.

Carol Let her try. Now, where were we? No, it's all right, I remember. You said Godfrey had been humbugging us both. But I thought you were his first wife.

Janet Oh, I was. But don't forget he has a mother. I take it you know her?

Carol Linda? Yes, of course. But he never called her a paragon to me.

Janet He didn't need to. He was holding me up to you instead. You lived with my image. I lived with my mother-in-law's.

Carol For crying out loud!

Janet (*getting maudlin*) The more he praised her wonderful qualities, the more I hated her. And all the time I'm sure she was a very nice woman.

Carol And you stood it for twenty years!

Janet Like you, I did my best, but it was no use. Compared to his mother, I was abominably extravagant.

Carol He told me you were economical!

Janet I'd no idea how to run a house. His mother's was like the Ideal Home Exhibition. I held him back in his career, whereas mother placed his feet on the first rung of the ladder with her charm and beauty. I didn't know how to entertain important people, but his mother could converse with kings and princes and hold them spellbound. You complain about being compared to me. You should have tried being compared to Linda.

Carol The hypocrite!

Janet Oh, I believed it entirely. I'd have gone on believing it if you hadn't told me how he described me to you. Now I wouldn't mind betting his mother was no better than either of us.

Mildred enters with the drinks

Is that my vodka?

Mildred It is, madam.

Janet Good. (*She opens her handbag*)

Mildred It is paid for, madam.

Janet I know, but this lady and I —(*she speaks very carefully*)— will have the same again. (*She puts a five-pound note on the tray*)

Mildred It's almost time for luncheon, madam.

Janet (*brightly*) So it is. How kind of you to remind me.

Mildred (*breathing heavily*) Not at all, madam.

Mildred goes

Carol We've made her day. (*She picks up her glass*)

Janet You've made mine. I'm so glad I met you. (*She picks up her glass*) Cheers.

Carol Cheers.

Janet (*after drinking*) This doesn't taste of anything.

Carol Watch it. It's stronger than it looks—And you put up with this treatment for twenty years?

Janet Twenty years and seven months. I even stayed on in this town because of the memory.

Carol And, of course, you were in love with him.

Janet Yes.

Carol And still are.

Janet (*loudly*) No! (*She hiccups*)

Carol But you said . . .

Janet That was an half an hour ago. The scales have fallen . .

(She hiccups again)

Carol Here, have some of my tonic water.

Janet (*enunciating carefully*) I don't want tonic water. I want my other vodka. (*She drains her glass*)

Carol I really don't think you ought to . . .

Janet I'm washing away the taste of twenty years of marriage to a monster.

Mildred enters with the drinks on her tray

Ah, here she comes, Sweet Nell of Old Drury.

Carol giggles. Mildred thoroughly alarmed puts the drinks on the table

(*To Mildred*) That's all for now, but hang about. We shall probably need you again.

Mildred tosses her head and exits quickly

Carol That's all very well, but . . .
Janet (*pouring tonic into the vodka*) What's all very well?
Carol What you were saying about the scales having fallen. But I can't help feeling that in telling you all this, I've done you a disservice.
Janet Nonsense.
Carol It's true. Until you met me you did at least have happy memories.
Janet I spent the best years of my life trying to please him.
Carol But you liked doing it. Before you found out who I was you were practically drooling over him.
Janet (*reflectively*) I suppose I liked it in a down-trodden sort of way. After all, he was everything I had. But at the end of it—when he left me—I was like a door-mat. Anybody could wipe their feet on me. You saw for yourself how Mildred treated me. Now, for the first time in twenty years, I'm beginning to think I could be a personality in my own right.
Carol Of course you could.
Janet Do you think somebody might give me a job?
Carol Why not? What can you do?
Janet Not much. I can keep house, of course, and cook and so on, but that's all.
Carol All! All! That would open dozens of doors to you. But what happens to Godfrey?
Janet What about him?
Carol I was counting on you to take him back.
Janet Do you care what happens to him?
Carol Not a bit.
Janet Neither do I. So he can go back to mother and the best of British luck to him.

They touch glasses and drink

Mildred enters and stands waiting

Shall we have another?
Carol No, I can't possibly. Nor should you.
Janet Nothing more then, thank you.
Mildred (*frostily*) I didn't imagine there would be, Mrs Talbot. I came to say there's another Mrs Talbot asking for you, Mrs Talbot.
Janet (*to Carol*) She's drunk.
Carol Don't be silly. It's ma-in-law. I phoned her to meet me here.
Janet Linda?
Carol Yes. (*To Mildred*) It's me, she wants. Tell her I'm in here. Oh, and bring a gin-and-French. That's her tipple.
Mildred (*nastily*) Just the *one*, madam?
Janet No, a vodka as well.
Carol No, you mustn't.
Janet I've got a few things to say to her. I shall never have the courage without it.
Carol If you have any more you won't be *able* to say it. (*To Mildred*) Just the gin-and-French.
Mildred (*fervently*) Thank *you*, madam.

Mildred goes

Carol Now you're not to be rude to Linda. I'm sure she didn't know what Godfrey said about her, any more than you did about me—I mean, I did about you. Oh, I don't know what I mean. But she's a very nice woman.

Linda enters. She is a smart woman in her sixties. She sees Carol first

Linda Carol, my dear, how lovely to see you.
Carol Thank you for coming, Linda.

Carol and Linda kiss

Janet (*quietly*) Hullo, Linda.

Linda looks across at Janet, for the moment not realizing who it is

Linda Why, if it isn't Janet. (*She goes to Janet*) How very surprising to find you here with Carol. I wasn't aware you knew each other.

Carol We didn't until about half an hour ago. It's Janet's day for her luncheon club. That's how we met in here. Now we're terrific friends.

Janet Companions in misfortune. (*She hiccups gently*)

Carol takes a chair from her table and places it above Janet's table, between herself and Janet

Carol I've ordered you a gin-and-French. It'll be here in a minute if the waitress hasn't collapsed from shock.

Linda (*looking at the glasses on the table*) Yes, you seem to have been having quite an orgy.

Janet More of a celebration.

Linda Of what?

Carol
Janet }Release from Godfrey { (*Speaking together*)

They shake hands across the table, smiling

Linda Well, I'm sure you both know what you mean, but I wish you'd put me in the picture. (*To Carol*) **Is** this something to do with your urgent telephone call to me?

Carol It is. To put it in a nutshell, I've left Godfrey.

Linda Behind or for good?

Carol For good.

Linda Oh.

Carol Aren't you surprised?

Linda Well—frankly, I'm not. To be truthful, I've been wondering lately how much longer it would last.

Carol (*to Janet*) I told you she was a nice woman.

Linda What exactly has been the trouble?

Carol Principally my failure to match up to Janet.

Janet Just as mine was my failure to match up to you.

Linda (*startled*) I beg your pardon?

Janet Oh, Linda, I meant to say such horrid things to you, but I can't. I don't really dislike you.

Linda I hope not, Janet.

Janet But, why, oh, why, did you have to be such a model of perfection?

Linda Model of perfection? Me? Don't talk rubbish. Whoever said so?

Janet He did. Your son. All the time.
Linda He couldn't have done!
Janet He did, I tell you. And I tried so hard.
Carol And he told me Janet was wonderful. And I tried, too, but not for so long.
Linda I'm utterly bewildered, though I understand now why you always avoided me, Janet, although we lived so close. But you're entirely wrong about Godfrey's opinion of me.
Janet Oh, no, I'm not.
Linda Oh, yes, you are.
Janet Oh, no, I'm not.
Carol (*to Janet*) Stop it. You're not a music-hall turn. Let Linda speak. Go on, Linda.
Linda Godfrey thought I was a terrible mother. He was always criticizing me.
Carol No!
Janet Oh, no!

Mildred enters with the drink

Mildred The gin-and-French for madam.

Linda reaches for her bag

It is paid for, madam.
Linda Thank you.
Carol That's all. You needn't wait.
Mildred Thank you, madam.

Mildred goes, relieved

Linda (*after a swig at her drink*) The times I've been grateful for alcohol. The marvel is that Godfrey never turned me into an alcoholic.
Carol (*astonished*) Linda, don't you like him, either?
Linda Not very much. No, that's an overstatement. I don't like him at all.
Carol I can't believe it.
Linda And he completely loathes me.
Janet He *adores* you.
Linda Rubbish. We can't stand the sight of each other. You've no idea how relieved I was when he married you, Janet.

Janet But—he's your son.

Linda That's my misfortune, dear. When he wanted a divorce from you I was terrified he might try and come back to me. Fortunately, he wanted to stay in town to be near Carol.

Janet But—you must have loved him once—I mean, when he was a baby.

Linda I wanted to, of course. But even when he was a child I could never do anything as well as Beatrice.

Janet Beatrice?

Linda And when he grew up he considered me a complete nincompoop.

Janet My head's going round.

Carol Drink your tonic, dear. (*To Linda*) Who was Beatrice?

Linda My elder sister. You never met her. She lives in the depths of the country now.

Carol How does she come into the picture?

Linda Well, you see, being a widow and having to earn my living, I was obliged to leave Godfrey to her. I saw him in the evenings, of course, and then it was absolute hell. I couldn't do anything right.

Janet But he couldn't have criticized you when he was only tiny.

Linda Couldn't he? Haven't you ever met a critical baby?

Carol There's no such thing.

Linda You didn't know Godfrey then. He was an angel in Beatrice's arms. When I took him up he yelled blue murder. He'd starve rather than let me feed him, but he'd take the whole bottle from Beatrice. Then when he was older, if *I* took him to the pictures, it was never a film he liked. If I bought him a book it wasn't nearly as interesting as the one Beatrice had bought him the week before. He reduced me to a nervous wreck.

Carol Well, I'm jiggered!

Linda Then, one day I tumbled to it. The little devil was playing me for a sucker. As soon as he was old enough, I packed him off to boarding school and arranged that Beatrice should have him for the holidays. We got along very nicely when we hardly ever saw each other.

Janet I'm absolutely flabbergasted. And I put up with him for twenty years.

Linda Yes. I must admit you had my complete and utter admiration. Though I did wonder at times, Janet dear, if you weren't a trifle mentally deficient.

Carol begins to laugh. It becomes a paroxyism

I don't think it's as funny as all that, Carol.
Carol Oh, but it is. The way he conned us all. And we all swallowed the bait, hook, line and sinker. But you have mucked up our little plan, Linda.
Linda What little plan?
Carol We were going to hand Godfrey back to you.
Linda To *me*! Perish the thought. I'd emigrate first.
Carol Well, he's bound to get in touch with you as soon as he finds my letter tonight, so you may have to.
Linda Unless he gets in touch with Janet.
Janet Oh no!
Carol Does he know you still live here?
Janet Of course he does. The alimony.
Carol Then it's action stations for all of us. I'd better find a nice anonymous hotel as far away from here as I can get. And you two had better . . .
Linda Wait a minute. I recently bought a little cottage in Scotland —well, it's not so little, really. And for some time now I've had the notion of setting up in business there.
Carol What sort of business? Highland tweeds or something?
Linda No, actually, I was thinking of opening it up as a teashop. It's right off the beaten track, but still likely to catch some of the hikers and mountain climbers.
Janet (*apprehensively*) Does Godfrey know about it?
Linda Don't be silly, dear.
Carol And Godfrey never walks!
Janet Or climbs mountains!
Linda That's why it occurred to me it might suit us.
Janet *Us*! Oh, Linda, may we come as well?
Linda Of course, if you'd like to.
Carol Like to!
Janet Oh, Linda!
Linda After all, I do owe you both something. I was responsible for Godfrey in the first place.
Carol I'll be your waitress. I'd be heaps better than that Gorgon. At least I'd smile at people.

Janet I make quite good scones. Well, other people think they're good, though Godfrey never said so.

Linda He only ate them. I know. Very well. we'll all go.

Carol Oh, what fun!

Linda Now let me see. There used to be a very good night train from King's Cross. You're packed, I see, Carol. Janet, you could throw a few things together?

Janet Easily.

Linda Then I don't see why we couldn't leave for a preliminary reccy tonight.

Carol And when Godfrey comes raging down . . .

Linda All the birds will be flown. We must think of a good name for our teashop, girls.

Janet *The Haven.*

Carol *Will Ye No Come Back Again?*

Linda I rather fancy *The Cuckoo's Nest*. Still, that's a detail we can settle later.

Mildred enters

Mildred (*to Janet*) The Luncheon Club ladies are assembling, madam.

Janet Oh yes, thank you. (*As Mildred turns to go*) Wait a minute. (*To Linda and Carol*) We've plenty of time for lunch before we need go. Why don't you both join us?

Linda Well, we have to eat somewhere.

Carol If you think they won't mind.

Janet Of course not. You're my guests (*To Mildred*) Ask them to lay two extra places, please. These ladies will be joining us.

Mildred (*seizing a lovely chance to be nasty*) It's extremely short notice, madam.

Linda It is rather, Janet.

Janet Leave this to me. (*Beginning quietly*) Mildred, have you enough plates?

Mildred Of course we have, madam.

Janet (*slightly louder*) And enough food?

Mildred Certainly.

Janet (*thundering*) Then lay two more places!

Mildred (*intimidated*) Very good, madam.

Janet And tell them to put a bottle of champagne at the Secretary's place!

Mildred (*thoroughly undermined*) A bottle of champagne. Yes, madam. Who shall they charge it to, madam?

Janet
Carol }Mrs Talbot! }(*Speaking together*)
Linda

Mildred stares, then slinks out

They all laugh

Carol Janet, you were magnificent. "Have you enough plates?" "Have you enough food?" Her face was a study.
Janet I suddenly felt emancipated. Or am I just drunk?
Carol Both, ducky.
Linda (*rising*) Leave your case here, Carol. It'll be quite safe.
Carol Linda, a thought has just occurred to me. Is Beatrice still alive?
Linda Certainly. She's only a year or two older than I am. Good heavens, do you think Godfrey will . . .
Carol I'm sure he will. Do you think she'll mind?
Linda I don't care if she does. It'll serve her right.
Carol Fancy being compared to the three of us. Poor Beatrice!
Linda (*laughing*) Poor Beatrice!
Janet (*rising, then moving a little uncertainly*) Poor—(*she hiccups*) —Beatrice!

Linda and Carol laugh, and each links an arm in Janet's. They go to door with her between them as—

the CURTAIN falls

FURNITURE AND PROPERTY LIST

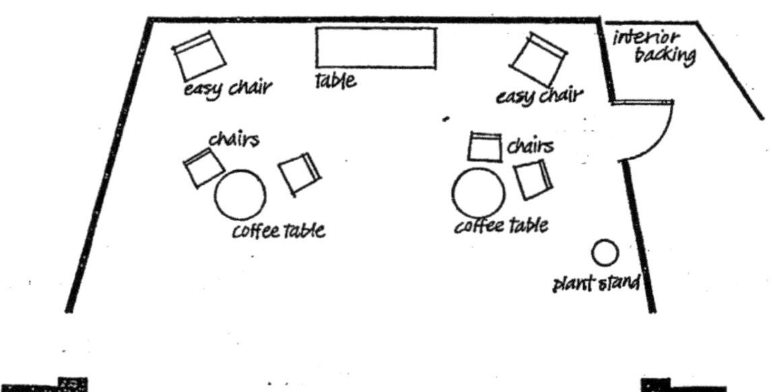

On stage: 2 coffee tables. *On one* (**Janet's**): coffee pot, cup, saucer, spoon, milk jug, sugar-bowl, ashtray

    Large table. *On it:* magazines, vase of wilted flowers

    4 upright chairs

    2 easy chairs

    1 plant stand

Off stage: Tray (**Mildred**)

    Suitcase (**Carol**)

    Gin-and-tonic (**Mildred**)

    Small sherry (**Mildred**)

    Gin-and-tonic (**Mildred**)

    Gin-and-tonic (**Mildred**)

    Vodka-and-tonic (**Mildred**)

    Gin (**Mildred**)

    Vodka-and-tonic, gin-and-tonic (**Mildred**)

    Gin-and-French (**Mildred**)

Personal: **Janet:** handbag with £5 note, watch

    Carol: handbag with cigarettes, lighter, £5 note, watch

    Linda: handbag

LIGHTING PLOT

Property fittings required: nil
Interior. A lounge. The same scene throughout
To open: General effect of midday light

No cues

MADE AND PRINTED IN GREAT BRITAIN BY
LATIMER TREND & COMPANY LTD PLYMOUTH
MADE IN ENGLAND